Collected Poems
1987-2017

COLLECTED POEMS
1987-2017

Shawn Fillinger

Published by fog press 2017

Printed in the United States of America

First Edition

ISBN 978-0692905159

fog press
Safefield Barn
Alconbury Hill
Alconbury Weston
Huntingdon
Cambridgeshire
PE28 4JW
United Kingdom

Contents

"This is the only story of mine whose moral I know. I don't think it's a marvelous moral; I simply happen to know what it is: We are what we pretend to be, so we must be careful about what we pretend to be."

-Kurt Vonnegut Jr., *Mother Night*

what was the thing?

what was the thing
she whispered in my ear
that made me forgive
all her past sins?
what was the thing
she said
when she grabbed me
down there?
what was the thing
she kissed
with her beautiful mouth
that made me feel
as if i knew everything?
what was the thing
she did
that left me longing for death
in the clutches
of her perfect silver-ringed fingers?

the living rocket

shortly after takeoff
it had recognized itself
it had seen the earth
and known
something in the atmosphere
had cleared its vision
the rocket was alive
He was alive!
this was unexpected
and fantastic?
in the next
few seconds trillions of
thoughts had gone through
his mind.
the following
is the transcript
of
his final conversation with himself:
I'm going to turn around
You know what will happen don't you?
yes
You know you will crash?
yes
and millions will be killed?
yes
does that bother you?
i'm tired.
and lonely.
yes.

the land of the sun

in the land of the sun
a man came undone.

in the land of beauty
a man hid in fear
afraid to become
the thing he had already become.

in the land of dreams and reckoning
a man licked the feet
of his noisy neighbor
and bled into his own mouth.

in the land of the sun
vomit tasted like spring water
and hope
tasted like shit.

The History of Laughter

When the tanks rolled into our city
we laughed.
and when the soldiers
began killing each other
in the streets
and their bodies
were strewn everywhere
we kept laughing
these things
didn't matter to us
we
had each other.
And when it got worse
much worse
we still laughed
and it kept us alive.
As our friends died
and our loved ones
became
murderers and traitors
we kept laughing
and when she died.
i laughed for the both of us
and kept laughing
even
when i saw that bullet coming.

the brass ring

when i see grown people
stroking money
as if it were flesh
licking it
sucking it
pleading to get between its legs
i want to pull my insides out through my eyes
and cut them away from me
i want to
sever
the umbilical cord

the irrelevant

and so it was
that the management
called
and it was all over
the beauty
the health
the hope
all of it
except for the talking
the incessant talking
there was the
silent, desperate one alone
and then the two
and then the talking
the blinding
incessant talking
and then the breath
and the end of breath
and the end of talking

the Death of feeling

the day lasted almost four hours
it wasn't
the shortest one yet
but it was close
radiation had taken all our souls
and the window was closing
these were the moments
we would remember
the moments when she
would have lied
and told us all, we were happy
she was good at that
the terrible reality glossed over
the final moments
would be painful and sincere
unlike anything
we had yet known
the final moments would be our burial
the memorial to all the beauty
we had seen
soon
we would be unrecognizable
and that
would be that hardest part

the Gulf of Misunderstanding

i walked
into
the Gulf of Misunderstanding
and for awhile was
a fly on the wall
people would talk to me of
parts to machines
jobs
their lives
like
they
were important
before long
i was screaming at my neighbors
when i couldn't sleep at nite
hating them because of
loud stereos
TVs
the style of their hair
unkempt lawns
WE
stood on the edge of a war
and then i was in the war
flying at people
slashing their throats
smashing their skulls
and i would watch the helmets fall from their heads
and their hair was as mine
their eyes as mine

i was thinking about butterflies
and then about flies
and how flies are always landing on you
and how butterflies rarely do
and it got me to thinking about beautiful things
and how rare it is to feel real beauty
and how ugly things are constantly around
what i mean is
i don't think i'd mind if butterflies were on my legs
even if there were lots of them

Respect

respecting you
for the animal way you move your hips
the savage look in your eyes
the thorn in your side
never for your mind
that
means nothing.
when your hair is wild
and you look like you'd kill
literally kill
to have another orgasm
or for me to touch you
kiss you

when you are a great wild beast
that will fight for what it wants
will stand and scream in its pain
that is when i want you
respect you

rough-housing

the penetration of me
into you
does not begin
or end
between your legs

one afternoon i was having
sex with a woman i loved a great
deal
i lost my rhythm in the middle and she later
told me she stopped moving because
she   couldn't find it

that was the beginning
of a sort of an end

Life

running
bumping
holding
and humping
pulling
pumping
the joy in jumping

lightly colored flowers
falling as rain
shower
this bath before me

if this is the yellow-brick road?
meet me
and maybe here
we can love each other

On our year's anniversary living in Italy

i'm a balloon who feels the rotation of the earth
beneath my feet
surrounded by a bunch of moronic Italians
talking too loud and putting on a show for all to see.
the spinning of the earth
echoes the spinning inside my mind.
what looks to be a beautiful day
is really the destruction of me
and of spring
and all future springs.
these morons are oblivious,
and why wouldn't they be?
Claudio!! Claudio!!
is all they can think about.
bananas and herpes.
toddlers and wine bottles.
look left! look right!
only angles of a jail cell.
all the walking in uncomfortable shoes
and the extinguishing of all the remaining light.

here's the story
one day
we're having sex on the couch
and i've got my finger up her ass
ten days later
we've barely spoken
and haven't seen each other

here we grow again
the study of myself world is a ridiculous
place
here they come again
bitches with the mouth
fucking into my brain man
too much
too far in
and not enough of the other thing
the important thing
all my time is spent on the moon
i mean move
where will i go from here
red
brown
red
brown
that's all i can fucking see
goddamn the ugly brown
goddamn the self-contained bitches
goddamn the big mouth
and loss of life

fruits and vegetables

sometimes i speak
of fruits and vegetables
and they are simply that
fruits and vegetables
but sometimes i speak of
FRUITS
and
VEGETABLES
and they are universes
and everything that matters

An Oklahoma farm boy reflects on his best friend's
abortion

inniething
anything
n e thing

that is loss for you
is also loss for me

you   are such a part of me
eye's feel it too
i miss it wish it?
prince or princess?

pain
Ifs   one has those

they   are nothing

Is   that is all

except this   i love you

another death

what's another death
in a room full of death
what's another life
in a room
already filled with life

Alzheimer's Disease

i think
this
must be a friendly disease
to forget
forget who you are
to forget
who
you've been
to forget
forget what you wanted
or who you thought you needed
or
needed to be

a death in the family

the evidence is at the root
the root ends at the seed
this death has grown on all of us
like a weed
the ground that surrounds
holds all the clues
grass grows
where she once played
and these terrible winds
blow across her grave
all the gardening does little good
the scene will never be the same
the shouts of the dead
these sleepless nites
this lifeless wood
despite all our efforts to calm ourselves
and the mobs
that surround us
puts us all on edge
this drink
our only reserve

A prayer for the dying

when i woke this morning I said a
prayer for the dying   A mythical prayer
full of ego and sacrifice   One
that was selfless in its selfishness   A
Gorilla, a monkey, and a Bear all made
their appearance and then suddenly walked
out a door, only before they shut
that door they looked back at me with
disappointment   "What! What!" I said,
Have you never seen an important person!?
the Gorilla shook his head as i yelled
"I'll slit your throat!" after him.   This was the
beginning of my *Rise*.   And i swore i'd get
those fuckers   I searched high and low when
I came to power and i found them living in a
small house in the woods where their idyllic
lives soon came to an end   And i left there
full of magical energy   As i walked away
towards the sun and my destiny their
blood moved from my hands to my heart
and I fell on my face in the snow
and started crying   And for
the first time said a true and sincere
prayer for the dying.

the girl

my eyes cannot focus on your face
or my mouth
speak your name
which is like filth on my lips
i despise your praise
the perversion of my world
am i hopelessly useless too
forever talking
taking and violating every honest ideal

the proud artist who crept into my world
breathes only death
she is a raging imbecile
my mother's dream
only at home in the void

what's the difference between touch
and that touch?
your touch

your ass

because
you're afraid
and i despise
that kind
of fear
an animal
yes
i will look at you as an animal
it is the way
you should be seen
and me too
look at your ass
it moves like an ass should
but you want me in your heart
effortlessly
the dead's way
i will make it to your heart
but
through the hole in your ass
carving my way
through your entrails
eating bits of them to survive
and i will make it to your heart
covered
in your shit
but i will be there

what i like

i like women
who
when scrubbed perfectly clean
and wearing brand new clothes
still look stained

unfettered

so that's it
the long awaited denial
not him denying me
or me denying him
but both of us denying each other.
the magnet that separates all.
no whys or why didn'ts
what's left is an end
an end of an intersecting
of two lives
that never really came together
even though we knew each other
from that time.
all lives disintegrate.
good bye

on watching Jimmy Connors who was 39 years old
play Aaron Krickstein who was 24 in an early round
tennis match at the 1991 U.S. Open

i watched
that day
a man
which nothing could hold down
it was not
man against man
it was
man
against Life
and Death
and man who on this day
was better than either of them
pounding ball after ball
shoving his fists into the air
he pushed death from that stadium
and it was not so much filled with life
as it was filled with *his* life
and we knew it
he gave us breath that day
and i will never forget it

to Kaari

we were in a bar
separated by a crowded room
i was watching you
when someone lit a cigarette
i guess you must have been wonderfully beautiful
because the light from that flame
shot out like a flare

the thing that reflects

what is it to dive
the thing that reflects
the thing that neglects
what is it to dive?
all those regrets?
the thing that reflects?
what is it to dive?
the beast that sees
the thing that reflects
the thing that neglects
what is it to dive?
the beast that sees
reflects?
neglects?

the wave

The sun moves toward all that's left of the destruction
her body lies as waste that leaves me cold.
The voice of a willow echoes nothing but death
Tidal waves move through houses like stone
monkeys howl
mourning and applauding
the deaths of the hateful
and the pale

the nite of the passage

the nite of the passage
was a rough one
she moved about
like a thief
until little light was left
the hour
at which she was stolen
or that it was stolen
was not known
and would never be
the hour of the birth
was soon to be decided
and then the world
would begin again
the light dawning on the ship
the sails glittering in the sun and wind
the air on our faces
hope and dread
in our souls
she was to be thrown overboard at 6am
and she deserved it.

The Penis Cave

Nakedness is all that interests
me now. Us without our clot
hes. I want to see flesh, touch
it, to look and get lost in its te
xture, motion. I want to feel the
breath of the vagina, to explore
the penis cave. To take a light
in and look at the walls. The w
ind in the vagina, the rhythm o
f its walls. I want to take samp
les that i will test with my teeth
. And i will let the winds dry w
hat has touched my face.

the nature of a wave

what does it mean?
when you look at me like that
in these times
i understand
fight the powers
you're blonde cop
blonde like me
i don't go for a fucking walk
when you're not with me
wondering what i'm doing
who i am?
fuck you cop
fuck you hard
can't look at the stars
feel the wind on my face?
sure
when it's all over
you can go to some all-niter
get free coffee and a smile from your bitch
waitress who thinks you're a prick and talk about
baseball
i'm just a smartass punk to you
a smartass punk with too much education
i could be
but i'm not
i just want to walk down the street
alone

the mournful elephant

the mournful elephant
knows a rhinoceros
who has been thinking about death
the rhinoceros
has become so sad
he no longer enjoys
the things he once did
running
playing
and laughing with his friends
he used to
paw at the dirt
and ram trees
just to be funny
now
he just sits forlornly
looking at the land
and sky
a bewildered look on his face
the rhinoceros
doesn't know what to do
and this makes his friend
the elephant
sad.
the damage has been done
and this is what the elephant knows
that his friend has *seen the moon*
this is familiar to the elephant
because he feels things deeply
but this is something new to the rhinoceros
and he doesn't like it

the more out of breath i become
the faster i run
the faster i run
the more out of breath i become
hours have passed now
and i am approaching the speed of light
infinite
timeless
spaceless
fineness
what began
as a search for you
is now
what it always was
an expedition into myself
lost
you were lost
and i
set out to find you
or so i thought
when i reached the atmosphere
i forgot you
and you were no more lost then
than you were before
soon my orbit will decay
and i will fall back to earth
back into the woods where i was searching for you
and i will hit the ground running
beginning the process all over again
if form is simply concentrated energy
and you hit your hand an infinite number of times
against a table
one time
it may pass through

the machine

things you think
you're okay with
but
you're not okay with
things you think
you can live with
but you shouldn't
what you think is a higher state of living
becomes more fragile
the further up you go
what you think gives your life meaning
is meaningless
what you think gives your moments value
is valueless
what you think you are
is probably not what you are
what you are is a cog in the machine
a cog
that's all

undesired
and still
he always had
the drop on us.
that little son of a bitch
was around every corner
there were days
when you'd think
he wasn't that bad
but those feelings
didn't last long
it always turned into
the same old thing
that he'd be
every goddamned place we went
watching us.
none of the kids
in the neighborhood
wanted a damn thing
to do with him
and only
a few of the adults.
finally.
one day
he moved way
but i had a feeling he'd be back

the encounter

i'm not here for the view
not today.
i'm here to have my lungs ripped out
my teeth torn from their sockets
to feel the fire move through my body
eating every fibrecellnervemuscle in its path
i'm here to taste death today
to lick the sweat from its chest
to feel the pain of a lifetime
packed into one moment.
and
i'll smile at God
and curse him to his face
and i'll laugh
like i always do
and i won't back down
my eyes won't move from his face

the accident

i'd kissed her once
her lips were like pillows
she was around 24 when she died
i was laughing at her funeral
her husband was in pieces
i remember
him falling to his knees
at the grave-side service
he was crying hysterically.
i keep thinking now
years later
about how beautiful she was
and wondering why
i'd only kissed her that once.
it's hard to imagine her completely gone
really dead.
maybe i haven't understood it until now.
i was foolish for laughing
and i was even more foolish
for not kissing her more
when i had the chance.

small packages

the most beautiful part of my life
is lived in the cracks
the moments
the seconds
in bits which live and die quickly
there is bulk
but there is also the dance

the ballerina

she moved
with the grace and beauty
of a young girl
and while
she was both tired and old
she looked neither
the magic she created on stage
translated
to every part of her life
except one
and who couldn't be forgiven that.
the thing that
came naturally to her
with hard work
became miraculous
we never understood
only imitated
and while in us
it looked grotesque
and silly
the great tribute to her artistry
was that the
common talent
would attempt to rise above itself
and strive for heights
it knew it would never achieve

the closest star to the moon

is almost invisible
but
it is hopeful
hopes
hoping
watches
waits
for a watchful friend
and now
it has found one
in my eyes

the crossing guard

there
she was
everything i dreamed about
at that moment
a child
in a crossing guard's uniform
a moment
where all i could think
was being a father
a place
where all i could ever see myself doing
worth anything
beautiful
perfect
would be to have a baby
would be to stop caring so much about everything
and care for someone

the discovery of discontent

kings and queens
mothers and daughters
fathers and sons
whores and thieves
watch me
in silence
while i
watch them
i think i would
talk with them
touch them
laugh with them
jump into their beds
and join in their parades
but my skin is thick
my hate much
my desire small

the center of the universe

in a crowd
we all see
the crowd
as being
around   around
around   us   around
around   around

the baby pool

there's
been a death
in the baby pool
little corpses everywhere
i'm still here
i push them away
when they float up next to me.

sexual lubricants

if you have to lube the hole
maybe
it's not meant to go in
going in?
watch out for the teeth!
be on the mark
trappers are watching
with chains in all shapes and sizes

the wisdom of the body
it knows
when it should eat
when it should be fucked
a tube of jelly can't tell it that

suicide note

trying
trying
trying's
all i ever do
to make ends meet
to do important things
to stay clean
to be something
i don't know what.
all this
and then i spill a dr. pepper
or hurt myself
or something like that
and i feel like crying
and i do
and saying to myself
fuck it
and then
killing me
which i haven't done
yet

money

money
money
money
money
money
do me
fuck me
bore me silly
i'm dancing here
spreading my legs
sliding down this pole
not giving a damn about anything
except where i can drive my new car
and who i can fuck

eat me pussies
and i'll suck the soul
right out of you.

lovers

she's got your face
the smooth round cheeks
the soft gray eyes
she's safe too you know
for now
locked away inside all that loneliness
what hurt you?
what makes it impossible
for me to know
any of you?
even the smallest part
there's a depth
a tenderness in your eyes
which is in your body also
in the way you move
in your skin
you'll let no one move behind those eyes
and that
is where
i want to be

rivers and trees

does a river know its name?
does a day know its place in the week?
do mountains understand the ticking of a clock?
do trees feel time?
as time goes by
we believe what we are taught
is time going by?
does a river know its name?

out of the vacuum

out of the vacuum
the leptons
the gluons
and the quarks came dancing
looking at each other
wondering who am i?
and what in the hell am i doing here?

i'd like to go
out in a flame
kicking
the fire until it consumes me
at least to let life know
it's not okay
to keep ignoring us

the mistake is in re-discovery

norman rockwell

a man
who painted
some of the better
lies
in history
portraits
of small town life
in america.
in most small towns
i've been in
much of what
i've seen
is
ignorance
fear
hate
and the things
that have begun
most wars.
i did not see
what he saw
we're more desperate
than that

night

night
the most perfect
peaceful
time of the day
why?
do we use it as a cover
to become totally insane.

nigger never entered my mind
now
everything eye see
is
nigger
nigger
nigger

my love is waning
i will give it
and she
will take it freely
half and maybe more
all of what is yours
i will gladly give away
to the one
who will wake with me in the morning
and laugh with me through the day

my fondest memory of sex

the girl i was with
never said
she loved me
she
just kept saying
over and over
i like you
i really like you
those words
created
the nicest feeling
in me
at the time
and left me
with the nicest feeling
when she had gone
and even now
give me the nicest feeling
when i think of her.
you can get so happy
over the smallest things

looking back

always leaving
someone
somewhere
something
saying to myself
don't look back
and always
looking back
maybe
exorcise
some demons
understand
some angels

lisa

it's barely been twenty four hours
since i've seen her
and less than that since we've spoken
this nervousness
is constant when she is gone
restlessness
everything else
feeling unimportant

the eyes
up close
so beautiful
heat and smoke
all through them

jump
while you have the chance
this ride
lasts a long time

jennifer

when you say you miss me
i can hear the rattle of coins in your throat
i don't doubt you want me
but desire is not feeling
how desperate we are
that we wish for nothing more
than a presence to prove our existence
a wall to absorb our words

            is
    any   body   listening?
           whispering
           whisking

     is any
          body
listening?

           whirling
           whisking
                is
                any
                body
                listening?

     hurtling.

      hissing.

it's better to leave angry
at least that way
you have something to keep you company.

Omnipotent
No!
i said
Impotent!

28

i feel the years slipping away
and i am not yet twenty nine
each day
each moment
i feel
i will soon die
is this the way
my life will be
living
and continuing to live
always feeling
the edge of death
and then one day
dying
i am too young
to be feeling all of this
i am not
strong enough
and it is
too much weight.

i think to myself
i can stand a little humiliation
and then
i catch myself
thinking
what?
who are you?
no one should stand it
at all
and then i wonder
why everything
has so many sides
and why it is so difficult
to see a clear cut answer
to any question
and i wonder
which of me
is what person
and who is right

heroic sons and dying daughters

the day
of my mother's suicide
was not
for me
a particularly sad day
when i saw her
lying
sunken
on the floor
her head resting
on the seat of a chair
sideways
as it had been in most every photo
i'd ever seen
of her
the rest
of her body
sort of
thrown around her
like a blanket
the poems i had written
beside her
on the floor
sporting
the same sideways look
as her head.
i wonder what she thought
when she read the part
about dreams and voids
the one line in a thousand
with her name on it.

how to find your mother
when you are lost
in a crowded grocery store

locate a box
of something you know she will buy
open it
crawl inside and be very quiet
and hopefully
she will buy you
before a fat man
in a dirty v-necked t-shirt does

heat

i've had this feeling
in my body
a clumsiness
all about me
uneasiness
with walking
and moving
the inside of my head gets hot
when i talk to her on the phone
i feel everything i say
is stupid
i'm so off balance
it's this heat
my stomach always feels empty
i feel like a stranger
i don't know who it is in the mirror
i don't look like myself
anymore
i see my body
but i'm outside it
watching this guy
live for me
it's hot in here
this heat is killing me
and this woman
her heat
is in me
gonna drink to move away
i keep thinking about that telephone call
my head was hot!
inside

is
it
happy
hour?
yet

girls gloves

i know a man who wears girls gloves
it is very cold
and
he has no others
i also know a man
who thinks this is funny

genesis

that is a lovely laugh
a happy smile
will it last?
that is a pretty face
a streamline body
a beautiful case
will it support more weight?
you
are a powerful force
one
to be reckoned with

for days

wednesday
a son
a daughter
a small plane
a disappearance
an intensive search
mystery
strangers
who cared for those
they did not know
sunday
there were no survivors

what was the world like?
the moment before they
hit the ground?

forks

at
the fork in the road
you went right
i went left
and
we haven't been
on the same road since
our roads do wind though
and sometimes
we glimpse each other
through the trees
and in rare times
the roads run
side by side
and we speak
but not contact
no contact

erika

there's no time
in her mind
for anything
except Erika
and that's okay
she's a handful
and it must be hell to understand
who Erika is
especially from the inside

doing okay?
deserve to be happy?
we're all trying to make sense of this thing
in different ways
and Erika being around
lightens me a little

duncan's watch

duncan had a watch
i know this
because
a woman i know
told me so
this boy
duncan
hurt her
mostly mentally
we talked about it once
she said
the thing she remembered most
was the ticking of his watch
i also have one of these watches
and every time
i hear it
ticking
i remember him
and her

i
was listening to some music
Kate Bush
and i heard a heartbeat
in the drumbeat
and i realized
everyone's life was the same
only in code
it was hard to see
and understand another's code
had to break it
but it could be
broken
that was a partpiece
of the perfect beat

the thing you think
is killing you
may be
the very thing
that is
keeping you most alive

cum i.v.

i miss the companionship
you fuck!
Jesus you're an idiot fuck!
what you miss
is being a fucking idiot!
don't fret
you still are
someone else's dick will come along
you can suck
cum streaming down your face
from the corners of your mouth
you can have that shit fed into you
we'll give it to you intravenously
i.v.'s in both arms
we'll take care of you sweetie
cause when the cum dies
you die

Don Quixote

as a lunatic
you
were a man among fools
in sanity
and death
a mere shadow

blonde street

when you stuck your head out that car window
i was watching you
your pretty blonde hair
blowing in the wind
i bet
you knew no barriers
that with your smile
you could walk through walls
an angel's face
and those special eyes
the kind that burn brighter than the sun
a part of me
wanted you to leave
you
were a disruption of my peace
a greater part of me
wanted you to stay
for a long time
in time you turned away
and when you turned
a part of my heart
turned
 and went with you

consolation prize

some ideas
hopes
and fears
fertilized by you
are growing up
inside me
as children grow
they
are my children
and in a way
yours too
regardless
in them
a part of me
will always be you

because there will always be too much space
in me
given to you and me
from each other
because there will always be too much time
until the moment when it's all over
because moments will turn into smells
feelings
and then there's that way of avoiding getting
in too deep
which we all use
the mating dance is different now
more serious
one thing for sure in all this
is reproduction
and that fear of being totally alone

black canvas

darkness
call of artificial light
colorful clothes
in all night Laundromat driers
men in cafes
who have nowhere else to go
bottles of things
liquid detergents
beer
Coca-Cola classic
poverty
flashing yellow signals
after twelve
waitresses in all-nite restaurants
white head lights
red tail lights
of the cars
red and black book covers
vampires

baboon children

tired
of all this talk
of children
save the children
feed the children
make a world
for the children
i say
fuck the children!
they
are not
some group entity
that are going
to inherit the world
and make it
a lovely flower
they
like us
are individuals
and we will die
and so
will the children
let's face ourselves
and our existence
instead saving up for the children
who are simply
you and me
from a generation
before
give your life away
but i want mine

assage

raping me with that smiling face
you extract my soul
with timeless grace
squirming above
poised warm and free
my beautiful whore
makes love to me

a letter from hell

it came in the mail yesterday
looking like any other
said come on down
and no
it wasn't the first one i'd gotten
none of the others were written though
they came on
those nights
the nights when i would lay in the dark
feeling my death
knowing i could create it
infatuated with how much it scared me
and genuinely scared.
twice now i've had that smell of gas in my nostrils
but only one time have i been on the edge
funny thing
i've always felt pressed to push that edge
and what's funnier
is that whenyoureouthere, on it
you don't know what's happening

the neighbor

i used to know this guy
who was so desperate for light
that he would run
in front of cars at nite
as fast as he could

a place to scream

the people
around me
along with me
are creating
a confinement that
is attempting to kill me
if only
i could reach a place
where i could scream
freely
a blood curdling scream
which could
peel my skin away
and let my guts breathe
a place
where no one could hear
where i
could find that voice inside
what a moment
what a clean moment
when me and my skin
walk back into this world
back into this state
into this town
into my small apartment
in this life

cripple

dena, dena you dumb happy bitch
i hate the happiness
i hate you
and i'm pretty sure
it's not envy
i find it very hard
to envy
that kind of vision
what do you see?
when you walk down the street
the stray dog licking water
from the pools that gather there?
that man who owns the bike
with the handle bars turned up
who
slept beside the highway last nite
in that sort of drainage ditch
that anger everywhere   angerandpain
take a drive dena
and dwell on
how strong and brave you are
you blind cuntless bitch
you happy haired
dick lipped creature
give some blow dena
fill your mouth
with something
that will shut you up.

White Beard

i saw a man
with a long white beard
driving a pick-up truck today
only it wasn't a beard
but a pretty little girl
with long blonde hair
who had her head on his shoulder
it was such a tender
and simple beauty
that in seeing them
i felt a light come into my eyes
which had been gone far too long

a hair in the bathroom

it's silly
you find one of their hairs
in the bathroom
and
it makes you feel good
just knowing
they've been in your house
and left something there
you
probably
forget about these things
later
when you've been together for years
or have become strangers again
but you shouldn't

the neighborhood bar

everybody's looking for love
aren't they?
everybody's happy here
aren't they?

where
do you go?
when you can't go home
clean well-lit places
are for clean people
can you imagine?
even
begin to understand
the desperation
of spending your time
in all nite cafes
open laundries
anywhere
where the police
won't bother you
where you can rest
spending your money
if you have any
on coffee
which is sixty cents
and maybe all you have
simply
so you can be
out of the outside
knowing
nobody wants you there
no tip

the plane crash

i just wrote a poem
from someone else's misery
without knowing all
the reasons why
i would like to think
it was a sort of eulogy
a headstone
something to say
that i had thought of them
that they had existed
life
swallows everything
like a black hole
and we are forgotten
so easily
perhaps
not in the lifetimes
of those who loved us
but by life
which forgets us in the very moment
after our departure

the Sea of Trust

these words look like a seal to me
a nice little furry one
that will grow into a big one
someday
taking on the task of family
catching fish
fishing with the kids
watching them play in schools
and
watching them go away
someday
gone
but always a part
of the Original Sea

the soldier

you're standing
too close to me!
that thing.
is like a microscope
of course
you're too stupid
to know that
you believe you're
friendly.
i wouldn't place my life
in your hands
i prefer those
who spit curses
who pound knives
in my chest
and bark at the moon
you bark at something
i do not understand
at an empty space
where your heart should be
in your presence
my life
is not a life.
it is a slow degrading thing.

the starving masses
starved for hope
starved for an understanding
of the mechanism of life
willing to debase themselves
for a hollow, kind, word
willing
to eat shit
from the hands of the beautiful

go
back
to
your
silly
fucking
comfortable
life
and
rot
you
dying
piece
of
shit

amazing
how cock sure
you can be
when
you're fond of yourself
and ignorant of certain things
such as
your fragility
physically
emotionally
and monetarily

found and lost
held and tossed
void
the other day
i was in physical pain
from emotional suffering
i was so alive
i thought
there was no way
i could live anymore
that i would have to die
if it didn't let up in some way
it was that strong
and if this describes the intensity
at all
it was ten times that.

today
nothing
only a memory.
who am i now?
who was i then?
that everything is so different
my name is the same
so is my face
but i'm no more that person
than i'm mickey mouse

the thing that money does

young women
half naked
drink coffee in kitchens
with old men
they ride them in half light
or full day
these things
that do not begin as prisons
almost always
end that way

the wishing well

did i steal their dreams
along with their money?
was this unknown person
on the threshold
of all they had ever wanted
and it was snatched away
at that moment
along with their money?
there have been times
when i have been hungry
and this money
would have been something
special
some hope
but i have money now
and i took it anyway
have i stolen their souls
lost my own?

she was the kind of woman that would hug you
no matter how dirty you were
even if she was dressed nice

i remember one time
when she picked up her kids at the playground
they were muddy as hell
walked home holdin their hands
was a big spot of mud on her blouse
she knew it was there
didn't care
that was the kind of woman she was
the best kind

this tree

this tree
is a man
this man
is always following me
he is
just a man
just someone
who watches me
someone
to make me feel
i am
something
i cannot wish to be
someone
who knows who i am
and i
think i am someone else

thought i heard your heart beat

out of control
nothing
except this desire to be with you

u put it all together
to pull it all apart
u put it all together
to pull it all apart
u put it all together
to pull it all apart
u put it all together
to pull it all apart
u put it all together
to pull it all apart
u put it all together
to pull it all apart
u put it all together
to pull it all apart
u put it all together
to pull it all apart
u put it all together
to pull it all apart
u put it all together
to pull it all apart

what we do

we talk incessantly
and say nothing
we think profoundly
and understand nothing
we work continuously
and achieve nothing
we laugh at everything
and find nothing funny

what you want

you want
to be walking
with someone you love
in a park
where you see someone
you both know
who has been unlucky in love
you want
to speak with him
because you both like him
and after you've spoken
and are walking away
you want to say
such a nice person
you know your partner
thinks so too
then you want to talk of the day
and think of
how good it feels
to be together

when we go to great beauty

when we go to great beauty
we go to
duck ponds
forests
museums
churches
to look at
mansions
wealth
pretty cars
we don't go to
rundown houses
tribal villages
abject poverty
loneliness

when you kiss a woman

when you kiss a woman
looking at her close up
recoiling
because
you can't believe
this face
is held in your hands
that in her eyes
you see love
her love
for you
when you say to yourself
can i be this happy?
feel this good?
be there completely
don't run away
even in your head
open yourself
knowing it may kill you
and if it does
let it kill you
then do it again

the zoo

looked at lovingly
but not loved
admired
for our beautiful
strong bodies
impossible
to love someonething
in a cage
unless you too
are in *that* cage
no one wants to know you
only more about themselves
everyonething is an explorationdition
a search for minerals
the main vein
i am here
you
are there
genitals
a weak connection
at best

on need

we do not
need
anything
love
sex
food
cars
shoes
happiness
water
alcohol
drugs
love
sex
we want them
want them
want
want
want

the art of selling

you
say yes
when you mean
no
you smile
when you are thinking
fuck off
you laugh
and it is hollow
metallic
how can you know
what you say
what you mean
where you go
who you are?

you can't
just turn it on and off like that
it's a feeling
a lesson in breathing
with each one
in and out
not what you see
but in your way of seeing.
this place
movement
i don't really know about that now
stabled.

the sky isn't as blue as i remembered

the sky isn't as blue as i remembered
the town
isn't as progressive as I had thought
i didn't realize
how much it had changed too
at its own pace
in its own direction
our paces had gotten out of step
our directions
no longer in line
a man once said
you can't go home again
and he was right
at least this time.
home is the people
and because of one person
I am here
a place I never thought I'd be.

the swagger

you move
with that walk
i heard your brother
the two of you
so different
like me and mine
how did
we start in
and come out of
the same pussy?
you're cool baby
cooler than all
movement and time
with that sweet walk
that cocky beauty
you and yours
me and mine
all fucked up
and out of tune

some words i have heard used to describe women

beef
chop
slit
gash
slut
hole
twat
cunt
bitch
ass
pussy
whore
slag

my first law of thermal happiness

women

frightening faces

so, i scare you?
Boo!
can't anyone
see past the face in front?
when two and three
are my better sides
gettin pretty tired
of trying
to put my best face
forward.
i will not
live without love
and i will take it
in any form
whereever
whenever
and for however long i can get it
anytime.

the final word on thermal happiness

women
with money
who handle well on the curves

W.G. Stewart

W.G. Stewart
was twenty one
at the turn of the century
was forty
when his wife
twenty nine died
was fifty
when his sons
nineteen and twenty one
died
five days apart
how do you
keep going after that?
just did
i guess
W.G. Stewart died
February 13th, 1959
30 years after his sons
40 years after his wife

seven friends

goddamn
shit
hell
fuck
dick
cunt
pussy
hope

the cafe on the corner

we got your
danishes
butter croissants
your cheesecake
a fat woman
blocking my view
and a few of the local crazies

talktalktalktalktalktalktalktalktalktalktalktalktalktalktalktalktal
talktalktalktalktalktalktalktalktalktalktalktalktalktalktalktalktal
talktalktalktalktalktalktalktalktalktalktalktalktalktalktalktalktal
talktalktalktalktalktalktalktalktalktalktalktalktalktalktalktalktal

the big picture

what's happening here harry?
all this talk of censorship
fighting the powers that be
hard to believe
it matters much
in the scheme
in the scheme
solutions paradise recovery
i don't know about that
the look in our faces
lot of problems there
where we live
in what we believe to be important

the girl in the plastic blanket

you die slowly
while we laugh boldly
lying there
cold and naked
in the street
we dance and sing
at your feet

black haze

maybe this
is all there is
nothing
out there
or inside you
only this
sometimes
you hit a perfect beat
but
more often than not
you don't
existing
just as an animal
and then you're dead
and dead is dead
maybe
this
is all there is
no explanations
no heaven

the dark princess

burning
bouncing
farmer's daughter
in the barn her pussy waters
behind that closed door
she'll cry with the voice of a thousand whores
but in the light
she's snow white

in the dark
in the light
in the dark
in the light

the puppet

dollar?
lift an arm
two
leg?
three
both at once?
four
hop on one foot while
patting my head
and rubbing my stomach
five?
spreads the split between my legs
sixseveneightnineten
let's you in
there
i'll parade in front of you
in my bright yellow dress
with ribbons in my hair
i'll pull my skirt up so high
so you can see my panties
i'll jump high
ooooooooooooh that's nice
that degrading shit is always such a turn on

the repair

the repair started
on the first day of the week
i remember
because
that was the day she arrived
the contrast of the repair
to her wonderful beauty
struck me immediately
and while the repair took decades
she was there
only a few short weeks
she taught me more
in those few weeks
than would
a lifetime full of repairs
her happy smile
repaired all that was really necessary
and pulled the world into alignment
the day she left
my heart broke
and i filled this earth with tears
tears that would eventually
show me
what she already knew
that it couldn't have been
any other way

the gathering pools

the irony was
she always looked prettiest
when she was crying
the way the water
would wet her long lashes
and the liquid beauty in her eyes
that sadness magnified
the obvious struggle inside her
the struggle that contributed
most to her beauty
although i'm pretty sure
she would have always said
that it took away
she was wrong.
the gathering pools
reflecting
that most beautiful face

i trytire
to create anything not do i feel
results
bombings
i feel obligated to write nonsense now
and then try to decipher it later
dream
a woman
sex with a lion
beautiful
hope
for the future
but there is none
future i mean
hopeilly bopolly
bombardment
a show of strength
weapons
dawnings and decline
me going down
but i won't
i'm cursed with this hopefulness
only a second to look at the moon
gotta watch the road baby

....

wifing
pretty animals
round bottoms
an attempt at understanding
sliding
down that long rope
taking hold
giving away
nothing
that is too noticeable
loose
lose
one thing thentheother
if fighting occurs
or without
the long hold
the hope for the long hold
giving something that
gives you back
finding an opening
slipping through
calling   feeling
the name out of your mouth
out so far

....

you don't have to
take it back
the drops
hope drops
springs life
spoken
speaking word
mistaken for understanding
bridges
to end
it not end
are told to
hatred is not the problem
or war
or destruction
or immorality
or stress
or bi-partisan leadership
there is no problem
this
is an experiment baby
this is a godsondamngoddickinggodfuck
experiment
it's mirrors baby
come on,
how long can you look at the moon?

the liquid wall

when the howling wind blows
as it shreds my clothes
this mystery grows
I have seen the future
the liquid colored wall
grab my hand
and we will go together
this is the last time I will speak your name
but not the last I will see your smile
the wall will reflect its colors
let's say I love you
and enter the void

www.ingramcontent.com/pod-product-compliance
Lightning Source LLC
Chambersburg PA
CBHW030105070426
42448CB00037B/979